2A

FOUR CORNERS

Second Edition   Workbook

T0159705

JACK C. RICHARDS & DAVID BOHLKE

CAMBRIDGE
UNIVERSITY PRESS

CAMBRIDGE
UNIVERSITY PRESS

University Printing House, Cambridge CB2 8BS, United Kingdom

One Liberty Plaza, 20th Floor, New York, NY 10006, USA

477 Williamstown Road, Port Melbourne, VIC 3207, Australia

314–321, 3rd Floor, Plot 3, Splendor Forum, Jasola District Centre, New Delhi – 110025, India

79 Anson Road, #06–04/06, Singapore 079906

Cambridge University Press is part of the University of Cambridge.

It furthers the University's mission by disseminating knowledge in the pursuit of education, learning and research at the highest international levels of excellence.

www.cambridge.org
Information on this title: www.cambridge.org/fourcorners

© Cambridge University Press 2012, 2019

First published 2012
Second edition 2019

20 19 18 17 16 15 14 13 12 11 10 9 8 7 6 5 4

Printed in Poland by Opolgraf

A catalogue record for this publication is available from the British Library

ISBN 978-1-108-56021-4 Student's Book with Online Self-Study 2
ISBN 978-1-108-57070-1 Student's Book with Online Self-Study 2A
ISBN 978-1-108-62772-6 Student's Book with Online Self-Study 2B
ISBN 978-1-108-62849-5 Student's Book with Online Self-Study and Online Workbook 2
ISBN 978-1-108-57586-7 Student's Book with Online Self-Study and Online Workbook 2A
ISBN 978-1-108-62779-5 Student's Book with Online Self-Study and Online Workbook 2B
ISBN 978-1-108-45958-7 Workbook 2
ISBN 978-1-108-45959-4 Workbook 2A
ISBN 978-1-108-45961-7 Workbook 2B
ISBN 978-1-108-65228-5 Teacher's Edition with Complete Assessment Program 2
ISBN 978-1-108-56039-9 Full Contact with Online Self-Study 2
ISBN 978-1-108-63454-0 Full Contact with Online Self-Study 2A
ISBN 978-1-108-68906-9 Full Contact with Online Self-Study 2B
ISBN 978-1-108-45968-6 Presentation Plus Level 2

Additional resources for this publication at www.cambridge.org/fourcorners

Contents

Credits

Photography

The following photographs are sourced from Getty Images:
U2: Walter McBride; Jon Kopaloff/FilmMagic; Junko Kimura; Kent Mathews; Steve Wisbauer; David Livingston; Matt Winkelmeyer; Jim Spellman; Munawar Hosain/Fotos International; **U3:** Furyphotographer; Tom Grubbe; Charles Gullung; Adam Burn; Zenshui/Laurence Mouton; Tetra Images; Danita Delimont; John Coletti; **U4:** Glow Décor; David Sacks/Digitalvision; Nicholas Eveleigh; Helen Ashford; Jamie Grill; Fuse; **U5:** Yuri Arcurs; Dorling Kindersley; Nopparatz; Antonio Guillem; **U6:** Karwai Tang; Johnny Nunez/Johnny Nunez; RichLegg; Andresr; Fpg; Bandian1122; Rick Rowell/Abc; James Devaney/Wireimage; John Lund/Annabelle Breakey/Blend Images; Grafissimo; Thinkstock; Erik Dreyer.

The following photographs are sourced from other libraries:
U1: Comstock/Media Bakery; Chris Ryan/Media Bakery; Daj/Amana Images Inc./Alamy Stock Photo; Aurora Photos/Alamy Stock Photo; **U2:** Rolf Bruderer/Media Bakery; Westend61 Gmbh/Alamy Stock Photo; Moviestore Collection/Rex Shutterstock; Everett/Rex/Shutterstock; Moviestore Collection Ltd/Alamy Stock Photo; **U3:** Media Bakery; Mike Kemp/Media Bakery; Gaertner/Alamy Stock Photo; Jason Lindsey/Alamy Stock Photo; Marshall Ikonography/Alamy Stock Photo; My Childhood Memories/Alamy Stock Photo; Photosani/Shutterstock; Ace Stock Limited/Alamy Stock Photo; Beaconstox/Alamy Stock Photo; Arco Images Gmbh/Alamy Stock Photo; Bob Gibbons/Alamy Stock Photo; **U4:** Luisa Leal Photography/Shutterstock; Dave Robertson/Alamy Stock Photo; William Milner/Shutterstock; Blend Images/Alamy Stock Photo; Natalya Bidyukova/Shutterstock; Mark J. Barrett/Alamy Stock Photo; Sourcenext/Alamy Stock Photo; Insadco Photography/Alamy Stock Photo; Karin Hildebrand Lau/Shutterstock; Ermolaevamariya/Dreamstime; **U5:** Kkulikov/Shutterstock; Ungor/Shutterstock; Art_Girl/Shutterstock; Kedrov/Shutterstock; Imagebroker/Alamy Stock Photo; Asia Images Group Pte Ltd/Alamy Stock Photo; **U6:** Tbs/Everett/Rex/Shutterstock; Amana Images/Alamy Stock Photo; Swell Media/Media Bakery; Viviamo/Shutterstock.

Illustration
QBS Learning.

Front Cover by Sergio Mendoza Hochmann/Moment; Betsie Van der Meer/DigitalVision; andresr/E+.
Back Cover by Monty Rakusen/Cultura.

My interests

A I'm interested in fashion.

1 Complete the puzzle and the sentences with words for people's interests.

Across

3 I'm interested in _____fashion_____.
   I like new and different clothes.

4 Tonya is interested in _____.
   She loves the old paintings at the museum.

8 Dennis is interested in _____.
   His favorites are Spanish, Portuguese, and Chinese.

Down

1 Mario is interested in _____.
   He likes basketball and soccer.

2 Jonathan is interested in _____.
   He works with the mayor.

5 Mrs. Wilson doesn't like _____.
   She hates computers!

6 Penny is interested in pop _____.
   She loves popular music and art.

7 Are you interested in _____?
   Let's go to China for a month!

2 Match the questions and the answers.

1 Where is Daniel from? ___e___   a Yes, she is.

2 How old is Ricardo? _____   b My name's Sophia.

3 Is he married? _____   c He's 24 years old.

4 Is she interested in literature? _____   d They're from Colombia.

5 Are you interested in travel? _____   e He's from Australia.

6 What's your name? _____   f I'm interested in pop culture.

7 Where are they from? _____   g No, he isn't.

8 What are you interested in? _____   h No, I'm not.

3 Look at Yolanda's information. Then answer the questions.

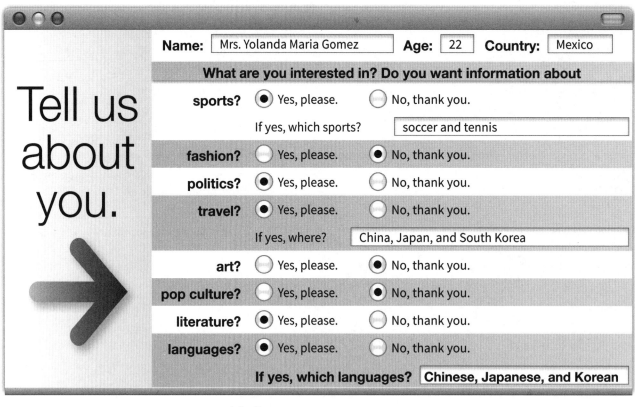

Tell us about you.

| Name: | Mrs. Yolanda Maria Gomez | Age: | 22 | Country: | Mexico |

What are you interested in? Do you want information about

sports?	● Yes, please.	○ No, thank you.
	If yes, which sports?	soccer and tennis
fashion?	○ Yes, please.	● No, thank you.
politics?	● Yes, please.	○ No, thank you.
travel?	● Yes, please.	○ No, thank you.
	If yes, where?	China, Japan, and South Korea
art?	○ Yes, please.	● No, thank you.
pop culture?	○ Yes, please.	● No, thank you.
literature?	● Yes, please.	○ No, thank you.
languages?	● Yes, please.	○ No, thank you.
	If yes, which languages?	Chinese, Japanese, and Korean

1 What's Yolanda's last name?   It's Gomez.

2 Is she married?

3 Is Maria her full name?

4 How old is she?

5 Where is she from?

6 What sports is she interested in?

7 Is she interested in Japanese?

8 What countries is she interested in?

4 Write about Yolanda's interests with the information from Exercise 3 on page 2.
Use the simple present of *be*.

1   Yolanda is interested in sports.

2   She's not interested in fashion.

3   _____

4   _____

5   _____

6   _____

7   _____

8   _____

5 Complete the conversation with questions.

Lynne Hello?

Judy Hello. This is Judy from *Speak Magazine*.
Can I ask you some questions?

Lynne Sure.

Judy Thank you. _____What's your name_____ ?
                                    1

Lynne I'm Lynne Roberts.

Judy Hello, Ms. Roberts. _____ ?
                                                        2

Lynne I'm from Chicago.

Judy _____ ?
                            3

Lynne I'm 31.

Judy _____ or single?
                            4

Lynne I'm married.

Judy _____ ?
                            5

Lynne My husband is 30 years old.

Judy _____ ?
                            6

Lynne Yes, we are. I'm interested in Spanish, and my husband speaks French.

Judy Great. _____ ?
                              7

Lynne Yes, we're interested in travel.

Judy OK. Are you and your husband interested in *Speak Magazine*?

Lynne Hmm . . .

B Can you repeat that, please?

1 Write the lines of the conversation in the correct order.

R-O-D-R-I-G-U-E-Z.
Hello, Gina. What's your last name?
Could you say that again, please?
Sure. Rodriguez.
✓ Hi. This is Gina.
My last name is Rodriguez.
Oh, OK, Ms. Rodriguez. How do you spell that?

Gina   Hi. This is Gina.

Clerk _____

Gina _____

Clerk _____

Gina _____

Clerk _____

Gina _____

2 Complete the conversations with *repeat* or *more slowly*.

1   **A**   It's on page 122.

    B   Can you say that _____ *more slowly* _____ , please?

2   **A**   What's your phone number?

    B   It's 324-555-1908.

    A   Could you speak _____ , please?

3   **A**   Her name is Na Young Park.

    B   Could you _____ that, please?

4   **A**   What's your last name?

    B   Lowery.

    A   Could you say that _____ , please?

5   **A**   The train is at 10:40 a.m.

    B   Can you _____ that, please?

C Do you play sports?

1 Label each picture with the correct word from the box.

baseball	golf	karate	swim	yoga
bowl	✓gymnastics	ski	table tennis	

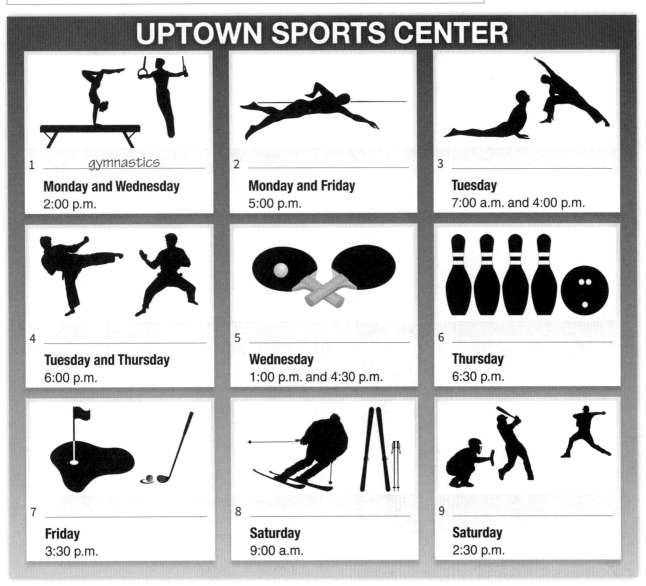

UPTOWN SPORTS CENTER

1 _gymnastics_
Monday and Wednesday
2:00 p.m.

2 _____
Monday and Friday
5:00 p.m.

3 _____
Tuesday
7:00 a.m. and 4:00 p.m.

4 _____
Tuesday and Thursday
6:00 p.m.

5 _____
Wednesday
1:00 p.m. and 4:30 p.m.

6 _____
Thursday
6:30 p.m.

7 _____
Friday
3:30 p.m.

8 _____
Saturday
9:00 a.m.

9 _____
Saturday
2:30 p.m.

2 Complete the sentences with the words from Exercise 1. Use *play* or *do* when necessary.

1 You can _____do gymnastics_____ on Monday and Wednesday at 2:00 p.m.

2 You can _____ on Wednesday at 1:00 p.m. and 4:30 p.m.

3 You can _____ on Saturday at 9:00 a.m.

4 You can _____ on Tuesday at 7:00 a.m. and 4:00 p.m.

5 You can _____ on Friday at 3:30 p.m.

3 Put the words in the correct order to make questions and answers.

1 play / does / she / What / sports / ?   A _What sports does she play?_
  table / plays / tennis / She / .   B _She plays table tennis._

2 gymnastics / they / do / Where / do / ?   A _____
  school / do / at / They / gymnastics / .   B _____

3 like / Does / he / karate / ?   A _____
  he / Yes / , / does / .   B _____

4 play / golf / When / do / you / ?   A _____
  the / golf / I / play / in / morning / .   B _____

5 you / Do / sell / skis / ?   A _____
  don't / No / , / we / .   B _____

6 they / afternoon / the / Do / swim / in / ?   A _____
  don't / No / , / they / .   B _____

4 Circle the correct words to complete the conversation.

Joe   Hey, Mari. Do you (like) / likes karate?
                     1

Mari   No, I **doesn't** / **don't**. I **like** / **likes** yoga.
                  2   3

Joe   **Do** / **When do** you do yoga?
       4

Mari   I usually **do** / **does** yoga after work.
                5

           Do / **What do** you like yoga?
           6

Joe   No, I **do** / **don't**. But my brother **like** / **likes** it.
           7   8

Mari   **Do** / **Where do** you like golf?
       9

Joe   Yes! I **play** / **plays** golf a lot. Do you
              10

           do like / **like** golf?
            11

Mari   Yes, I **do** / **does**.
           12

Joe   Great! Let's play golf on Saturday.

Mari   OK.

5 Complete the text with the simple present forms of the verbs in parentheses.

MINIATURE GOLF
SCORECARD

HOLE	Linda	Debbie	HOLE	Linda	Debbie
1	3	4	10	3	4
2	5	5	11	1	3
3	2	3	12	2	3
4	7	4	13	3	4
5	4	6	14	5	4
6	4	2	15	3	2
7	5	4	16	4	5
8	3	3	17	1	4
9	6	6	18	4	3
			Total	65*	69

Linda _____likes_____ (like) the game miniature golf. A miniature golf course
1
_____ (have) 18 holes, but the course is very small. At the end of
2
the game, the person with the lowest score _____ (win).
3
Linda _____ (play) miniature golf with her friend Debbie. They
4
_____ (play) in the park on Saturdays, and Linda usually
5
_____ (win) the game. But that's OK with Debbie.
6
She _____ (like) the game, too, and they always
7
_____ (have) a lot of fun.
8

6 Read the text in Exercise 5. Use the answers below to complete the questions.

1 _What game does_____ Linda like?   miniature golf
2 _Does a miniature golf course have_____ 18 holes?   Yes, it does.
3 _____ with?   with her friend Debbie
4 _____ miniature golf?   in the park
5 _____ miniature golf?   on Saturdays
6 _____ the game, too?   Yes, she does.

7 Answer the questions about a sport you like.

1 What is the sport? _____
2 When do you play it? _____
3 Where do you play it? _____

7

D Free time

1 Read the text. Check (✓) the events that are in a decathlon.

1 ✓ the 100-meter run   4 ☐ the 500-meter run

2 ☐ the high jump   5 ☐ the low jump

3 ☐ the 1500-meter hurdles   6 ☐ the long jump

The decathlon is a sports competition with ten different events. Athletes compete in all ten events for two days. After the ten events, the person with the best score wins.

There are four races, or track events, in the decathlon: the 100-meter run, the 400-meter run, the 1500-meter run, and the 110-meter hurdles. In the 110-meter hurdles, athletes run and jump. Athletes also compete in six field events. In the long jump, people run and jump. In the high jump, they run and jump over a high bar. In the pole vault, athletes run and jump over a high bar with a long

pole. In the shot put, the javelin throw, and the discus throw, athletes throw different things. The shot is a large heavy ball. The javelin is a long thin pole. The discus is like a large round disk or plate.

The women's decathlon started in 2001. Before 2001, only men competed in the decathlon. Women now compete in the same ten events, but there are some differences. For example, the hurdles are lower and women jump over hurdles on a 100-meter course, not on a 110-meter course, like the men's decathlon. The shot, the javelin, and the discus in the women's decathlon are not as heavy as in the men's events.

2 Read the text again. Rewrite the sentences. Correct the underlined words.

1 The decathlon has <u>twelve</u> events.   *The decathlon has ten events.*

2 Athletes throw things in <u>five</u> events. _____

3 The shot is a large heavy <u>disk</u>. _____

4 <u>Women</u> jump over hurdles on a 110-meter course. _____

5 The <u>men's</u> decathlon started in 2001. _____

Descriptions

A He's talkative and friendly.

1 Put the letters in the correct order to make personality adjectives.

1 i y f l d r n e   _____friendly_____
2 v i t t k a a e l   _____
3 n i d f n e c t o   _____
4 n s u e o g r e   _____
5 y s h   _____

6 v c e i r t a e   _____
7 n u y f n   _____
8 g d n k w h r r a o i   _____
9 r s s u i e o   _____

2 Complete the sentences with some of the adjectives from Exercise 1. Use the simple present of *be*.

1 Ethan ____is shy____ but ____confident____ .

2 Rita _____ and _____ .

3 Tom and Ed _____ and _____ .

4 Paul and Yoko _____ _____ .

5 Ms. Perez _____ _____ .

6 Emma _____ _____ .

3 Rewrite the sentences with the words in parentheses.

1 Laura is shy but confident. (person)
   Laura is a shy but confident person.

2 Sue and Kelly are hardworking. (students)
   _____

3 Dana is talkative and funny. (girl)
   _____

4 He's serious but friendly. (guy)
   _____

5 She's generous. (mother)
   _____

6 They're creative and confident. (musicians)
   _____

7 I'm friendly. (person)
   _____

8 Mr. Nelson is talkative but serious. (teacher)
   _____

4 Complete the conversation with *What . . . like?* questions.

Doug Hi, Isabel. How's your art class?

Isabel I love it! My teacher is Mrs. Linden.

Doug _What's she like_____ ?
         1

Isabel She's great. She's creative but serious. There are 12 students in the class.

Doug _____ ?
         2

Isabel They're shy, and they're not very friendly. But my friend John is in the class.

Doug _____ ?
         3

Isabel John is a talkative guy.

Doug And _____ ?
             4

Isabel Me? I'm a serious and hardworking student!

5 Read Part 1 of Jenny's job evaluation. Then complete the evaluation in Part 2 with the simple present and the correct adjectives.

ACE ACCOUNTANTS
EMPLOYEE EVALUATION FORM

Employee's Name: Jenny Lewis   Job: Accountant   Date: May 24

Part 1: Which words describe the employee? Check the words.

☑ serious   ☑ confident   ☑ hardworking   ☑ creative

☐ talkative   ☐ funny   ☑ shy   ☑ friendly

Part 2: Write an evaluation of the employee.

Jenny ___is a serious___ accountant and very _____ . She
          1   2
_____ . She works late every day. Jenny _____ person
          3   4
and has many good ideas. She is not very talkative or funny. Jenny _____
                                                                        5
but _____ . People like her.
        6

6 Write conversations for the pictures with your own ideas. Use *What . . . like?* questions and *be* + adjective (+ noun).

Examples: **A** ___What are they like?___   **A** ___What's he like?___
          B ___They're friendly and funny.___   **B** ___He's a confident and creative actor.___

Tina Fey and Amy Poehler, comedians

Johnny Depp, actor

1 **A** _____ ?   2 **A** _____ ?

   B _____ .   **B** _____ .

7 Write conversations for another actor or actress, singer, or musician.

1 Actor or actress: _____   2 Singer or musician: _____

   A _____ ?   **A** _____ ?

   B _____ .   **B** _____ .

B I don't think so.

1 Circle the correct sentence to complete the conversation.

1 A Is Mia hardworking?

   B **I think so.** / **I don't think so.** She always works late.

2 A Does your teacher give a lot of homework?

   B **I believe so.** / **I'm not really sure.** It's the first day of class.

3 A Is Jay-Jay talkative?

   B **I guess so.** / **I don't believe so.** He's shy.

4 A Are Mr. and Mrs. Trandall generous?

   B **I believe so.** / **I don't believe so.** They sometimes help me.

2 Look at the pictures. Complete the conversations with expressions from Exercise 1.
   More than one answer is possible.

1 A Is Larry funny?

   B _I don't think so. / I don't believe so._

2 A Does Paula take a dance class?

   B _____

3 A Are Tina and Jordan friendly?

   B _____

4 A Does Eric like baseball?

   B _____

C What do they look like?

1 Match the descriptions with the people in Joe's family. Then write about them.

A	B	C	D	E
young	middle-aged	bald	middle-aged	short and
tall and thin	long blond hair	a gray mustache	curly hair	overweight
wavy shoulder-	little round	elderly and	a short black	young
length hair	glasses	medium height	beard	straight black hair

1 This is my mother.
    She's middle-aged.
    She has long blond hair.
    She has little round glasses.

2 This is my grandfather.

3 These are my brothers.

4 This is my sister.

5 This is my father.

2 Read the clues and label the pictures with the correct names.

- Ken's hair isn't straight, long, or brown.
- Megan doesn't have short or black hair.
- Diane's hair isn't brown.
- Mario's hair isn't long or blond.

  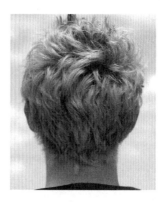 

long black hair   short brown hair   wavy blond hair   straight blond hair

1 _____   2 _____   3 _Ken_____   4 _____

3 Answer the questions. Use the information from Exercise 2.

1 What does Ken look like?   He has wavy blond hair. _____
2 What does Mario look like?   _____
3 What does Megan look like?   _____
4 What does Diane look like?   _____

4 Look at the answers. Write the questions with *What . . . like?* or *What . . . look like?*

1 What does he look like? _____   He has a brown mustache.
2 What's he like? _____   He's confident and serious.
3 _____   She has long straight hair.
4 _____   They're tall and overweight.
5 _____   They're friendly and talkative people.
6 _____   I'm short and thin.
7 _____   He's pretty funny.
8 _____   I'm creative and hardworking.
9 _____   We have curly red hair.

5 Complete the chart with the words from the box.

black	curly	green	long	new	round	straight	wavy
blond	elderly	✓ little	middle-aged	red	short	tall	young

Size	Age	Shape	Color
little			

6 Put the words in the correct order to make sentences.

1 hair / straight / John / has / brown / .   _John has straight brown hair._

2 short / He's / a / elderly / man / .   _____

3 round / Wendy / glasses / has / little / .   _____

4 have / eyes / green / They / small / .   _____

5 beard / long / He / a / has / gray / .   _____

6 We / hats / blue / new / have / .   _____

7 Look at the pictures. Write sentences. Use some of the words from Exercise 5.
More than one answer is possible.

1 _He has short brown_
   hair.
   He's young.

2 _____
   _____
   _____
   _____

3 _____
   _____
   _____

4 _____
   _____
   _____

D People's profiles

1 Read the text. Write the name of the artist and the cartoon under the correct picture.

1 _____

2 _____

3 _____

Famous Cartoonists

Jim Davis

Jim Davis is famous for his comic strip, *Garfield*. It's about a cat named Garfield. This cat is lazy and eats a lot of lasagna. Garfield also sleeps a lot. Jim's comic is about a cat. Jim played with lots of cats when he was a boy, and he has a pet cat and a dog now. This helps him draw and write about Garfield. Jim lives and works in Albany, Indiana.

Matt Groening

Matt Groening is famous for the cartoon *The Simpsons*. The characters in *The Simpsons* have the same names as the people in Matt's family, but they don't look like his family. The father in the cartoon, Homer, is bald. The mother, Marge, has big blue hair. They have three children. The sister, Lisa, is extremely serious, and Maggie is a baby. Bart is talkative and funny. Matt says Bart is like him. Matt is from Portland, Oregon, but he lives near Los Angeles, California now.

Cathy Guisewite

Cathy Guisewite also lives in California, but she's from Dayton, Ohio. For 34 years she wrote a comic strip called *Cathy*. *Cathy* is about a woman's life. She and her mother do not always see things the same way. In the cartoon, Cathy likes to eat, and her mother thinks she's overweight. Cathy also has problems at work. The real Cathy is retired, and she has one daughter.

2 Read the text again. Then circle the correct answer.

1 Jim's cartoon is **Garfield** / *The Simpsons*.

2 The cartoon of Marge **looks like** / **doesn't look like** Matt's mother.

3 In *The Simpsons*, Lisa is very **serious** / **talkative**.

4 **Jim and Cathy** / **Matt and Cathy** live in California now.

5 The real Cathy has a **daughter** / **son**.

Rain or shine

A It's extremely cold.

1 Label each picture with the correct word from the box.

cloudy
✓cold
cool
hot
rainy
snowy
sunny
warm
windy

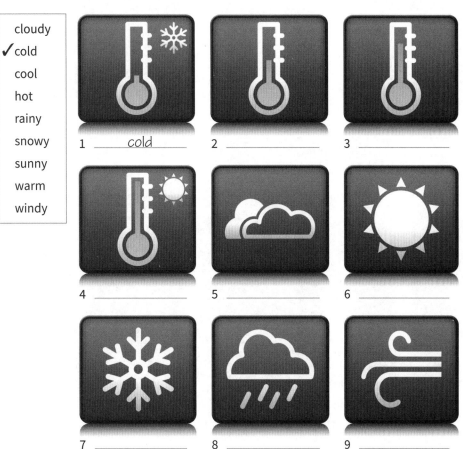

1 _cold_
2 _____
3 _____
4 _____
5 _____
6 _____
7 _____
8 _____
9 _____

2 Look at the map. Write sentences about the weather. Use the simple present of *be* and words from Exercise 1.

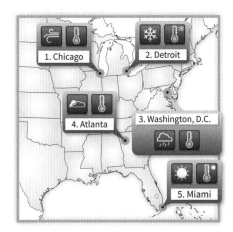

1. Chicago
2. Detroit
3. Washington, D.C.
4. Atlanta
5. Miami

1 _It's windy and cool in Chicago._
2 _____
3 _____
4 _____
5 _____

3 Circle the correct answer for each picture.

1 What season is this?

   a It's warm.

   b It's the rainy season.

   (c) It's the dry season.

2 What season do you like?

   a I like summer.

   b I like winter.

   c I like fall.

3 What season is it now?

   a It's the dry season.

   b It's the rainy season.

   c It's snowy.

4 What season is it in Toronto?

   a It's winter.

   b It's spring.

   c It's summer.

5 What's your favorite season?

   a It's fall.

   b It's winter.

   c It's the rainy season.

6 What season does he like?

   a He likes sun.

   b He likes winter.

   c He likes spring.

4 Cross out the word that doesn't belong in each list.

1 extremely	really	~~fairly~~	very
2 somewhat	a lot	pretty	fairly
3 summer	spring	sunny	fall
4 cold	warm	snowy	cool
5 summer	windy	snowy	rainy
6 cloudy	winter	sunny	snowy

5 **Put the words in the correct order to make sentences.**

1. very / winter / It's / cold / the / in / .   _It's very cold in the winter._
2. spring / lot / in / It / rains / a / the / .   _____
3. New York City / windy / It's / pretty / in / .   _____
4. in / cool / It's / fairly / Quito / .   _____
5. season / in / It / dry / much / doesn't / rain / very / the / .   _____
6. summer / in / at / snow / It / doesn't / all / the / .   _____
7. a / It / Canada / bit / snows / quite / in / .   _____
8. extremely / It's / Bangkok / in / hot / .   _____

6 **Circle the correct words to complete the sentences.**

1. It's **pretty** / **a little** sunny today.
2. It rains **pretty** / **a lot** in London.
3. It's **extremely** / **a lot** hot in Istanbul.
4. It's **somewhat** / **very much** cool in March.
5. It doesn't snow **somewhat** / **very much** in Sydney.
6. It's **very** / **a lot** cloudy in Seattle.
7. It doesn't snow **extremely** / **at all** in Lima.
8. It's **at all** / **fairly** windy in Iceland.
9. It rains **a little** / **very** in December.
10. It's **really** / **quite a bit** hot in Mexico City.

7 **Write about the weather in your town. Use the words in parentheses.**

Example: (snow) _It snows a lot in the winter._ or _It doesn't snow at all._
1. (snow) _____
2. (rain) _____
3. (windy) _____
4. (hot) _____
5. (sunny) _____
6. (cloudy) _____

B In my opinion, . . .

1 Complete the conversations with the words from the box.

| I'd opinion think thoughts what what's |

A. **Rosa** Hey, Marcos. Let's have a party for Mom.

  Marcos OK. When?

  Rosa Hmm . . . I don't know. _____What_____ do you think?

           1

  Marcos I _____ Saturday is a good day.

     2

  Rosa OK. That sounds good.

B. **Jake** Hi, Todd. When are you coming to see me?

  Todd Well, I'm not sure. What are your _____ ?

           1

  Jake In my _____ , winter is a good time. It usually

      2

  snows a lot. We can ski!

  Todd OK. That would be great.

C. **Hiro** So, Julie. When is a good time for you to visit?

  Julie _____ say in the winter. It's cold and snowy here.

     1

  Hiro OK. Where should we meet?

  Julie Hmm . . . _____ your opinion?

        2

  Hiro How about Kyoto? Then you can meet my parents. It's somewhat cool in
  the winter, but it doesn't usually snow.

  Julie That's a great idea!

2 Match the pictures to the conversations in Exercise 1. Label the pictures with the correct conversation letter.

1 ☐

2 ☐

3 ☐

C I'd like to play chess.

1 Complete the sentences with a word from each box. Use the simple present form of the verbs.

bake	✓do	make	play
do	make	play	take

a board game	✓a jigsaw puzzle	a video	cookies
a crossword	a nap	chess	popcorn

I usually _do a jigsaw puzzle_ with
_____
     1
my children.

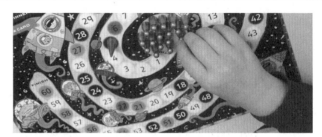

Sometimes, we _____
                        2
with friends.

Sometimes, my wife and I _____
                                    3
_____ on Friday evenings.

But we always _____
                        4
on Sunday mornings.

On Sunday afternoon, the kids _____
                                        5
_____ .

And my mom _____
                        6
for us.

My wife _____ .
                        7

And I sometimes _____
                        8
like this one.

21

2 Look at the chart. Then answer the questions.

Healthy Pines Recreation Center

Activities for Wednesday Afternoon

NAME	PLAY CHESS	PLAY A BOARD GAME	DO A JIGSAW PUZZLE	BAKE COOKIES	DO YOGA
Ethan			✓		
Carolyn	✓				
Paul	✓				
Marina				✓	
Emma		✓			
Doug		✓			
Jenny					✓
Mark					✓

1 What would Ethan like to do?   <u>He'd like to do a jigsaw puzzle.</u>

2 Would Carolyn and Paul like to play chess?   <u>Yes, they'd like to play chess.</u>

3 What would Marina like to do?   _____

4 Would Emma like to bake cookies?   _____

5 Would Doug like to play a board game?   _____

6 What would Jenny and Mark like to do?   _____

3 Look at the answers. Write the questions about the underlined parts.

1 <u>What would she like to play?</u>   She'd like to play <u>a board game</u>.

2 _____   He'd like <u>to take a nap</u>.

3 _____   I'd like to play <u>baseball</u>.

4 _____   <u>No, they wouldn't</u>. They don't like gymnastics.

5 _____   I'd like to do yoga <u>in the park</u>.

6 _____   <u>Yes, she would</u>. She loves chess.

7 _____   <u>No, I wouldn't</u>. I never take naps.

8 _____   They'd like to make a video <u>at the school</u>.

4 Write sentences about what the people would like and wouldn't like to do.

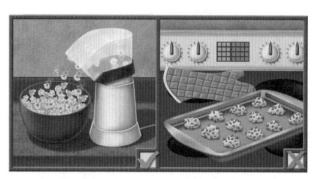

1 Kara _would like to play table tennis._
She wouldn't like to play soccer.

2 Dan _____

3 Sheila and Greg _____

4 Mr. and Mrs. Jones _____

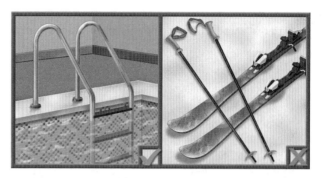

5 Larry _____

6 Claudia _____

5 Answer the questions with your own information.

1 Would you like to play chess tonight? _____
2 Would you like to take a nap on Saturday? _____
3 Would you like to play soccer tomorrow? _____
4 Would you like to do your homework in a park? _____
5 Where would you like to go for vacation? _____
6 When would you like to go to bed? _____

D Where would you like to go?

1 Read the email. Write the names of the places and the weather under the correct pictures.

1 _____Otavalo_____   2 _____   3 _____   4 _____

_____cool_____

_____pretty cold_____

Hi, Rachel!

I'm having a great time in Ecuador with my family. We're in Quito right now. It's the capital of Ecuador. The city is big, and there's a lot to do. It's warm in the day and cool at night now. It sometimes rains a lot in Quito, but it's not the rainy season now. We're walking around the city a lot.

The weather is really different in other parts of Ecuador. In the town of Otavalo, the weather is cool all day and pretty cold at night. There's a famous market in Otavalo with many handmade clothes. We went to Otavalo on Monday. We got beautiful sweaters at the market to wear at night!

There are a lot of beaches in Ecuador. The beaches are usually sunny and very hot. We went to a beach in Muisne on Wednesday and had a great time! It was sunny and hot!

Cotopaxi National Park is close to Quito. The park is very big, and it has a large volcano in it. The volcano is also called Cotopaxi. It snows quite a bit on Cotopaxi, and it's extremely cold and snowy at the top. You can walk to the top. The kids can't do it, but Helena and I would like to walk up there this weekend.

How are you? Say hi to Mike and the kids.

Your friend,
Martin

---

2 Read the email again. Then write T (true), F (false), or NI (no information).

1 Quito is the capital of Ecuador. ___T___

2 There isn't a market in Quito. _____

3 Martin and his family liked the beach in Muisne. _____

4 Martin's children are very young. _____

5 Martin and Helena are in Cotopaxi National Park now. _____

6 Rachel would like to go to Ecuador. _____

Life at home

A There's a lot of light.

1 Cross out the word that doesn't usually belong in each list.

1 **bedroom:** dresser closet ~~dishwasher~~
2 **bathroom:** sink sofa shower
3 **living room:** armchair coffee table toilet
4 **kitchen:** bathtub refrigerator cupboards
5 **bedroom:** curtains stove bed

2 Complete the sentences with some of the words from Exercise 1.

STUFF FOR SALE →

I'm selling my ___bed___
                    1
and _____ . They're
              2
two years old. $150.

For sale: an old

_____ . $50.
       3
Email r27@cup.org.

We're selling our

_____ and
            4
_____ . Click
       5
here to respond.

House for sale. Two bedrooms,
a big _____ with a
              6
dishwasher.

I can make _____ for
                  7
your bedroom or living room!
Call Susie at 222-5678.

I can fix your _____
                        8
and _____ !
              9
Email Jason at Jfix@cup.com.

3   **What's in your home? Complete the chart with the words from the box.**

Example: Kitchen   _three cupboards, a sink, a refrigerator_

armchair	closet	curtains	refrigerator	sink
bathtub	coffee table	dishwasher	shelves	sofa
bed	cupboards	dresser	shower	stove

Living Room	Kitchen	Bedroom	Bathroom

4   **Write about your home. Use *some*, *a few*, *many*, and *any* and the words in parentheses.**

Example: _There are a few cupboards in my kitchen._   or
           There aren't many cupboards in my kitchen.

1 (cupboards / kitchen) _____

2 (shelves / bedroom) _____

3 (armchairs / living room) _____

4 (closets / house) _____

5 (bedrooms / house) _____

5   **Circle the correct word or phrase to complete each sentence about Sandra's house.**

1 There's **a lot of** / **many** noise on the street.

2 There's **some** / **a few** light in the living room.

3 There isn't **many** / **any** space in the closets.

4 There's **a little** / **a few** light in the bedroom.

5 There aren't **many** / **a little** cupboards in the kitchen.

6 There are **much** / **a few** shelves in the bathroom.

6 Complete the questions with *much* or *many*.

1 How _____much_____ light is there in the kitchen?

2 How _____ closets are there in the bedrooms?

3 Are there _____ shelves in the closets?

4 How _____ street noise is there?

5 Is there _____ space in the kitchen?

7 Complete the conversation with the questions from Exercise 6.

Mr. Clark So, this is the house for sale.

Andrew Oh, it's nice. _How much street noise is there?_
                                                    1

Mr. Clark Oh, it's fairly quiet.

Lydia Now about the house!

_____
                        2

Mr. Clark There's quite a bit of light.

Andrew That's good. We love cooking.

_____
                        3

Mr. Clark No, not really. It's pretty small, but there are a lot of cupboards.

Lydia And the bedrooms? _____
                                                    4

Mr. Clark There are two closets in the big bedroom, and there's one closet in the small bedroom.

Andrew Oh, that's good. _____
                                                    5

Mr. Clark I'm not sure about the shelves. Let's look at the house!

Lydia That's a good idea!

8 Read the answers. Then write the questions.

1 _How much noise is there in the living room?_   There isn't any noise in the living room.

2 _____   There is some light in the bathroom.

3 _____   There are a lot of cupboards in the kitchen.

4 _____   There isn't much space in the dresser.

5 _____   There are a few shelves in the bedroom.

6 _____   Yes, there are four armchairs in the living room.

B Can you turn down the music?

1 Check (✓) all the words that complete the request.

_____ you open this cupboard, please?

- ✓ Could
- ☐ How
- ☐ When
- ☐ Where
- ☐ Would
- ☐ Do
- ☐ Can

2 Check (✓) all the responses to the request in Exercise 1.

- ✓ No problem.
- ☐ Oh, really?
- ☐ A little.
- ☐ In my opinion.
- ☐ Sure.
- ☐ I'd be happy to.

3 Complete the request and the response in each conversation. Use different words and expressions from Exercises 1 and 2.

A. **Karen** Hey, Jeff. It's Karen from upstairs.
Would you turn down

1
your TV, please? It's too noisy, and I'm studying.

Jeff _____.

2
Sorry about the noise.

Karen Thanks.

B. **Tessa** It's hot in here.

Megan I know. _____

1
the window, please?

Tessa _____.

2

Megan Thanks. That's better.

C. **Don** Hey, Liv. _____

1
the phone?

Liv _____.

2

Don Thanks. I can't talk right now.

28

C I always hang up my clothes!

1 Complete the household chores with *away*, *off*, *out*, or *up*.

1 wipe _____off_____ the counter
2 take _____ the garbage
3 hang _____ the clothes
4 clean _____ the yard
5 drop _____ the dry cleaning
6 pick _____ the magazines
7 put _____ the dishes
8 clean _____ the closets

2 What household chores can you do with these items? Label the pictures with some of the phrases from Exercise 1.

1 _clean up the yard_

2 _____

3 _____

4 _____

5 _____

6 _____

3 Rewrite the sentences.

1 Please pick up those magazines.   _Please pick those magazines up._

2 Can you take out the garbage?   _____

3 Dennis cleans his yard up every week. _____

4 I usually put away the dishes at night. _____

5 Would you drop this letter off at the post office? _____

6 My son and daughter never hang their clothes up. _____

4 Complete the answers with the phrasal verb and *it* or *them*.

1 Where do you drop off your dry cleaning?   I _____ _drop it off_ _____ at Super Clean.

2 Where do you hang your coat up?   I _____ in the closet.

3 Who can clean up the living room?   David can _____ .

4 Who can clean out the closets?   Marta and Vern can _____ .

5 Do your children put away their toys?   No, they don't _____ .

6 Does your husband take the garbage out?   No, I _____ .

7 How often do you wipe off the counters?   I _____ three times a day.

8 How often does Miho clean the garage out? She _____ once a year.

5 Rewrite the questions in Exercise 4 with *it* or *them*.

1 _Where do you drop it off?_

2 _____

3 _____

4 _____

5 _____

6 _____

7 _____

8 _____

6 Look at the chart. Who does each chore? Write two sentences about each chore.
Use *it* or *them* in the second sentence.

	Sunday	Monday	Tuesday	Wednesday	Thursday	Friday	Saturday
1. put the dishes away				Kelly and Tim			Dad
2. take out the garbage			Dad			Kelly	
3. drop off the dry cleaning		Mom				Tim	
4. pick up the dry cleaning	Kelly			Dad			
5. hang the clothes up			Kelly		Tim		
6. clean up the yard		Mom and Kelly					Dad and Tim
7. clean up the bathrooms			Mom and Tim			Kelly	
8. clean out the cars	Kelly and Tim			Mom and Dad			

1   Kelly and Tim put the dishes away on Wednesday.   Dad puts them away on Saturday.

2 _____   _____

3 _____   _____

4 _____   _____

5 _____   _____

6 _____   _____

7 _____   _____

8 _____   _____

7 Answer the questions with your own information. Use *it* or *them*.

1 Who takes out the garbage in your home? _____

2 How often do you wipe off the counters in your kitchen? _____

3 When do you put away the dishes? _____

4 How often do you drop off the dry cleaning? _____

5 Where do you hang up your clothes? _____

6 How often do you clean up the kitchen? _____

D What a home!

1 Read the article. Then complete each sentence with one word.

1 Jake: "When I travel, my bed is on a _____."

2 Maria: "When I travel, I sleep in a _____ bed."

3 Tom and Riana: "The virtual _____ is very clean."

Other Homes

Do you have another place you call "home"? Four people describe their "other homes."

JAKE LONDON'S TOUR BUS

I'm a musician. I play the guitar and sing. I travel quite a bit with my band, so my other home is a big bus. There's a kitchen and a bathroom on the bus. There's a small living room with a TV. There are six beds on the bus, one for each person in the band!

MARIA MILLER'S HOTEL ROOM

I'm a flight attendant. Because of my job, I stay in hotels a lot. The hotel rooms usually have a big bed, a small kitchen, and a desk. So, hotel rooms are my "other homes." I always bring a few personal items when I travel for work. I take a nice dress, a few T-shirts, and my favorite jeans. I take a small pillow, and I always take a good book. I'm usually in one place only for a day, so I can put my things away in five minutes!

TOM AND RIANA PETERSON'S VIRTUAL HOUSE

Our "other home" isn't real! We love computer games. We play a game on our computer in a virtual world. We have avatars in this virtual world, and they have a home! Our real home is a small apartment, but the virtual house is big. In the virtual home, our avatars do the household chores. They clean up the rooms, put away the dishes, and take the garbage out. The virtual house is very clean, but our real house is a mess!

2 Read the text again. Answer the questions.

1 What does Jake do? He's a musician.

2 Is there a TV on Jake's bus? _____

3 What does Maria do? _____

4 How much time is Maria usually in one place? _____

5 Who does the household chores in Tom and Riana's virtual home? _____

Health

A Breathe deeply.

1 Label the parts of the body with the correct words from the box.

ankle	eye	hand	leg	nose	teeth
arm	finger	✓head	mouth	shoulder	toe
ear	foot	knee	neck	stomach	wrist

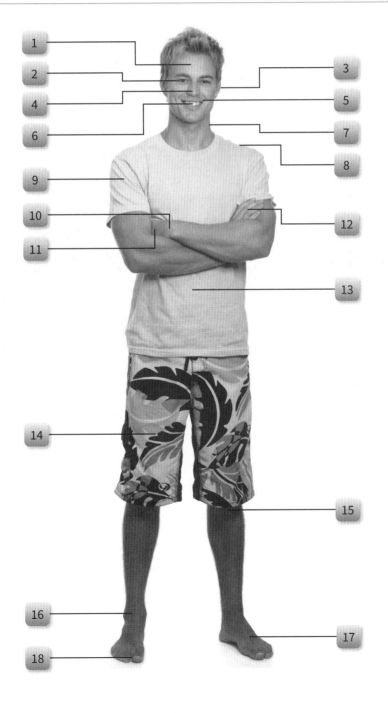

1	head
2	
3	
4	
5	
6	
7	
8	
9	
10	
11	
12	
13	
14	
15	
16	
17	
18	

2 Match the objects to the corresponding parts of the body. Label each picture with the correct word from the box.

✓back	eyes	feet	finger	neck	wrist

1 _____back_____   2 _____   3 _____

4 _____   5 _____   6 _____

3 Complete the instructions with the correct form of the verb in parentheses.

TIPS for Using Crutches

1 _____Walk_____ (walk) slowly.

2 _____ (not look) down.

3 _____ (wear) good shoes.

4 _____ (practice) with a friend.

5 _____ (not walk) on snowy streets.

6 _____ (not open) doors.

_____ (ask) a friend for help.

7 _____ (have) a friend move chairs and tables in your home.

8 _____ (be) careful!

4 Complete the chart with the correct adverbs.

	Adjective	Adverb
1	careful	carefully
2	deep	
3	heavy	
4	noisy	
5	quick	
6	quiet	
7	slow	

5 Circle the correct adverb to complete each sentence.

1 Raise your arms _____ .

   a noisily   b deeply   (c) quickly

2 Please talk _____ in the library.

   a slowly   b quietly   c noisily

3 Walk _____ , please. I can't walk quickly.

   a heavily   b slowly   c quietly

4 Don't talk _____ . The baby is taking a nap.

   a noisily   b slowly   c heavily

5 Lower your head _____ .

   a heavily   b noisily   c carefully

6 Breathe _____ in yoga. Relax and breathe slowly.

   a deeply   b noisily   c quickly

6 Write sentences with the words in parentheses. Use the simple present or the imperative form of the verbs and the adverb form of the adjectives.

1 Jim stretches slowly. _____ (Jim / stretch / slow)

2 _____ (breathe / deep / for ten minutes)

3 _____ (not breathe / heavy)

4 _____ (Millie / talk / quiet / on the phone)

5 _____ (not walk / quick / after lunch)

6 _____ (we / listen / careful / to our teacher)

7 Answer the questions with your own information.

Example: _I talk quickly._ or _I talk slowly._

1 Do you talk slowly or quickly?   _____

2 Do you drive quickly or carefully?   _____

3 Do you walk quietly or noisily?   _____

B I'm not feeling well.

1 Complete the puzzle with words for health problems. What's the mystery word?

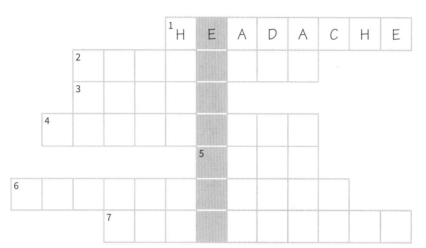

Crossword:
1. H E A D A C H E

1   2   3   4

5   6   7

2 Complete each conversation with two different expressions from the box.

Get well soon.	I feel awful.	✓ I'm not feeling well.
I don't feel so good.	I hope you feel better.	Take it easy.

A. **Ed** Hi, Pat. How are you?

   Pat I'm not feeling well. _____
                              1

   Ed What's wrong?

   Pat I have a bad cough.

   Ed That's too bad. _____
                             2

B. **Meg** Hey, Tim. How are you?

   Tim _____
                              1

   Meg What's wrong?

   Tim I have the flu.

   Meg Oh, no! _____
                             2

C How healthy are you?

1 Put the letters in the correct order to make phrases about healthy habits.

1 tae a ablnadec tide
   eat a balanced diet

2 ttpeocr uyor sink
_____

3 tea a ogod fraeskbat
_____

4 tge gnhueo pesel
_____

5 sreeecxi idyla
_____

6 shaw yrou dashn
_____

7 og rfo a klwa
_____

8 flit gwsieth
_____

2 Look at the pictures. How often do you do these things? Write sentences about your habits using some of the phrases from Exercise 1 and *always*, *usually*, *hardly ever*, or *never*.

Example: _I usually eat a balanced diet._

1 _____

2 _____

3 _____

4 _____

5 _____

6 _____

3 Complete the questions with *How long, How many, How much, How often,* or *How well.*

1 <u>How many</u> vegetables do you eat at dinner?   Hmm . . . Not many.
2 _____ do you walk in the mornings?   For about 30 minutes.
3 _____ do you play soccer?   Pretty well.
4 _____ meals do you cook a week?   Ten meals.
5 _____ coffee do you drink each day?   Two or three cups.
6 _____ do you do karate?   Once a week.
7 _____ do you do yoga?   For about an hour.
8 _____ sleep do you get?   Quite a bit.

4 Look at Greg's answers to an online health quiz. Write the questions.

ARE YOU HEALTHY?
Choose the answers that best describe your habits.

1 **Q:** <u>How often *do you eat breakfast?*</u>

   A: I eat breakfast *every day*.

2 **Q:** _____

   A: I follow my diet *pretty well*.

3 **Q:** _____

   A: I exercise *daily*.

4 **Q:** _____

   A: I drink *a lot* of water.

5 **Q:** _____

   A: I *don't get much* sleep.

6 **Q:** _____

   A: I wash my hands *three times* a day.

7 **Q:** _____

   A: My eating habits are *somewhat healthy*.

8 **Q:** _____

   A: I spend *four hours a day* at the gym.

5 Write questions with *How* and the words in parentheses to complete the conversation. Use the answers to help you.

Tae Ho Hi, Fran. How is your mom feeling?

Fran She's not well. She's always tired and doesn't eat well.

Tae Ho <u>How much fruit *does she eat?*</u> (fruit / eat)
                                             1

Fran A lot. She eats apples or bananas every day.

Tae Ho _____ (eat / vegetables)
                              2

Fran She always eats vegetables at dinner.

Tae Ho _____ (meals / eat / a day)
                              3

Fran Two. Breakfast and dinner. Is that OK?

Tae Ho Well, three is better. _____
             (go to the gym)   4

Fran About three times a week.

Tae Ho _____ (spend at the gym)
                              5

Fran Oh, about an hour. She lifts weights, and she does yoga.

Tae Ho _____ (sleep / get)
                              6

Fran About four hours a night.

Tae Ho That's not much sleep. In my opinion, that's why she's always tired!

6 Rewrite the questions from Exercise 5 with *you*. Then answer the questions with your own information.

1 <u>How much fruit *do you eat*</u> ?
   I _____ .

2 _____ ?
   _____ .

3 _____ ?
   _____ .

4 _____ ?
   _____ .

5 _____ ?
   _____ .

6 _____ ?
   _____ .

D Don't stress out!

Read the text. Write the instructions from the box in the correct places.

Move your arms to the right.	Sit carefully on the ball.
Raise your body.	Then lower your head and arms.

The New **HealthyYou** Exercise Ball

Repeat these exercises 20 times for each activity.

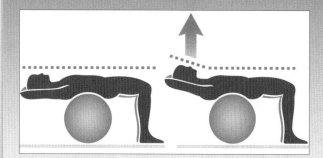

THE SIT UP

1 Put your back carefully on the ball. Place your feet on the floor.

2 Put your hands behind your head.

3 Raise your head and arms slowly. Hold your stomach in.

4 _____

THE WEIGHT LIFT

1 _____
   Place your feet on the floor.

2 Hold a weight in each hand.

3 Lift the weights over your head. Keep your back straight.

4 Lower the weights to your shoulders.

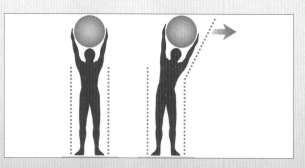

THE REACH

1 Stand up and hold the ball. Stretch your arms and raise the ball over your head.

2 Move your arms to the left. Keep your legs straight. Don't move your feet.

3 _____

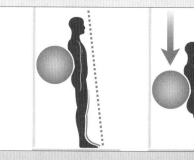

THE SQUAT

1 Place the ball against the wall. Put your back against the ball.

2 Lower your body, bending your knees. Keep your back straight.

3 _____

What's on TV?

A I love watching game shows.

1 Look at the pictures. Circle the correct answer.

1 What type of shows do
  they like?
  (a) Documentaries
  b Cartoons
  c Talk shows

2 What type of shows does
  Jim watch?
  a Reality shows
  b Sitcoms
  c Cartoons

3 What's his favorite type of
  TV show?
  a Game shows
  b The news
  c Soap operas

4 What do they watch
  at night?
  a The news
  b Talk shows
  c Dramas

5 What type of shows does
  his family watch?
  a Sitcoms
  b Documentaries
  c Game shows

6 What does Sarah watch
  after work?
  a Sitcoms
  b Dramas
  c The news

7 What's on TV?
  a A game show
  b A cartoon
  c A talk show

8 What's that?
  a A cartoon
  b A reality show
  c A soap opera

9 What are they watching?
  a The news
  b A drama
  c A talk show

2 Complete the chart. Write the verbs from the box in the correct column.

dislike	✓hate	like	prefer
enjoy	hope	love	want

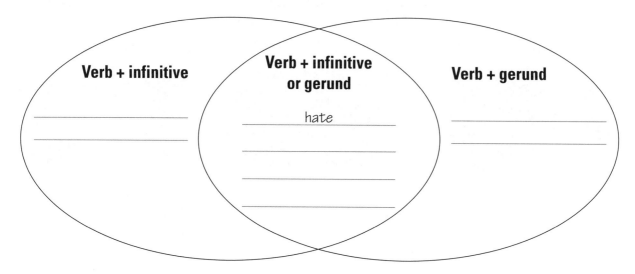

Verb + infinitive

_____

_____

Verb + infinitive or gerund

_____ hate _____

_____

_____

_____

Verb + gerund

_____

_____

3 Put the words in the correct order to make sentences.

1 at night / shows / watch / I / like / reality / to / .

   I like to watch reality shows at night.

2 to / new / Melvin / buy / TV / next week / hopes / a / .

   _____

3 on the Internet / TV shows / dislikes / My / mother / watching / .

   _____

4 do / What / love / of TV shows / types / watching / you / ?

   _____

5 favorite / hate / We / our / missing / show / .

   _____

6 on the radio / listen / Sarah and Mike / prefer / to / to the news / .

   _____

4 In four of the sentences from Exercise 3, the verb can be followed by either a gerund or an infinitive. Rewrite those sentences in the other way.

1 _____ I like watching reality shows at night. _____

2 _____

3 _____

4 _____

5 Answer the questions with the words in parentheses. Use the correct form of the verbs. Sometimes two answers are possible.

1 What shows do you watch on TV?

  I love watching sitcoms. / I love to watch sitcoms. _____ (love / watch / sitcoms)

2 Does your sister like reality shows?

  Yes. _____ (enjoy / watch / them)

3 Do you listen to the radio?

  No, I don't. _____ (prefer / listen / to music on my computer)

4 Why is Jack at the store?

  _____ (want / buy / a new TV)

5 Why is Laura at the bookstore?

  _____ (hope / see / that famous writer)

6 What types of movies does Paul like?

  _____ (like / watch / dramas)

7 Why aren't Dan and Susan at the mall?

  _____ (hate / shop)

8 Do you and Mary watch a lot of TV?

  No. _____ (dislike / watch / TV)

6 Circle the correct words to complete the conversation.

Mara Hey, Ken. What's wrong?

Ken   Well, I **hate** / **dislike** to watch TV.
      1

Mara Oh, OK. What do you **enjoy** / **want** to do?
      2

Ken   Hmm . . . Well, I **like** / **want** riding bikes.
      3

Mara But it's really cold outside!

Ken   You're right. I **hope** / **enjoy** playing board games.
      4

Mara Well, I **prefer** / **enjoy** to play chess.
      5

Ken   OK. Let's play chess! Could you turn off the TV?

Mara Well, actually . . . I **want** / **dislike** to watch it
      6
      while we play.

Ken   Oh, no!

B I don't really agree.

1 Complete the conversation with *agree* or *disagree*.

Tim   I think cartoons are great!

Aisha   I _____agree_____ . They're funny!
                        1

Wendy   I don't really _____ , Aisha.
                                       2

Cartoons aren't funny. They're boring.

Aisha   Wendy, don't you like soap operas?

Wendy   Yes, I do. Why?

Aisha   Well, I think soap operas are boring!

Wendy   I _____ . They're interesting!
                        3

Tim   I'm afraid I _____ , Wendy.
                              4

They are pretty boring!

Wendy   Well, what do you think of reality shows?

Tim   Oh, they're great . . . interesting and funny!

Aisha   I _____ with you, Tim!
                        5

Wendy   Hey, I think so, too. Let's watch a reality show.

2 Complete the conversations with your opinion. Use some of the expressions from Exercise 1.

A. **Tim**   I think cartoons are great.

   Aisha   I think so, too. They're funny.

   You   _____
                                    1

   Wendy   I think cartoons are boring.

   You   _____
                                    2

B. **Aisha**   Do you like soap operas?

   Wendy   Yes! I think soap operas are interesting!

   You   _____
                                    1

   Tim   I think soap operas are boring!

   You   _____
                                    2

44

C I'm recording a documentary.

1 Complete the sentences and the puzzle with television words.

Across

2 Jenny likes to watch _____ of old sitcoms on TV. She watches the same shows from the 1990s every night.

5 Do you _____ the sad parts of movies? I never watch them.

6 I'm going to work. Can you _____ my favorite show? Thanks!

7 I like watching TV shows online. I _____ through the boring parts!

Down

1 I don't pay for any TV channels, but there are some good shows on _____*public*_____ TV.

2 Where's the _____ control? I want to turn the TV on.

3 Do you have _____ TV? You have great channels, but I didn't see a dish outside.

4 I hate watching TV. I like the shows, but I don't like the _____ .

2 **What are they doing on Saturday? Read the sentences. Label the pictures with the correct names.**

- Tom is staying home on Saturday.
- Tonya is taking her school books to the library on Saturday.
- Isabella is going to a club on Saturday.
- Randy is playing a sport on Saturday.
- Emily is driving to her sister's house on Saturday.
- Mateo is meeting a friend at a Japanese restaurant on Saturday.

1 _____Isabella_____   2 _____   3 _____

4 _____   5 _____   6 _____

3 **Match the questions and answers. Use the information in the sentences and the pictures in Exercise 2.**

1 What's Tom doing on Saturday? ___e___   a He's playing soccer.

2 What's Randy doing on Saturday? _____   b He's eating sushi with Naoki.

3 What's Isabella doing on Saturday? _____   c She's visiting her sister in San Francisco.

4 What's Emily doing on Saturday? _____   d She's doing her homework at the library.

5 What's Mateo doing on Saturday? _____   e He's watching TV.

6 What's Tonya doing on Saturday? _____   f She's going dancing.

4 Rewrite the sentences. Use the present continuous and the words in parentheses.

1 She goes to work.
    _She's going to work on Monday_____. (on Monday)

2 He watches reruns of his favorite TV show.
    _____. (tonight)

3 What do you do for fun?
    _____? (this weekend)

4 Does he teach English in South Korea?
    _____? (next year)

5 We don't record our favorite shows.
    _____. (on Friday)

6 The Hawks play the Lions.
    _____. (next week)

7 I don't cook Mexican food.
    _____. (for the party)

8 Where does she travel for work?
    _____? (next month)

5 Look at some of Becky's plans for next week. Then read the answers and complete the questions.

Thursday	Friday	Saturday	Sunday
- buy a new TV	- have a party for Mark - make and post a video of the party	- watch the baseball game with Tim - record the game for Doug	- visit my parents - go out with Joan

1 _Is Becky buying a new TV_____ on Friday?   No, she isn't. She's buying it on Thursday.

2 _____ on Sunday?   No, they aren't. They're watching it on Saturday.

3 _____ on Saturday?   No, she isn't. She's having it on Friday.

4 _____ of the game?   No, she isn't. She's making a video of the party.

5 _____ for Mark?   No, she isn't. She's recording it for Doug.

6 _____ on Thursday?   No, they aren't. They are going out on Sunday.

7 _____ her grandparents?   No, she isn't. She's visiting her parents.

8 _____ on Saturday?   No, she isn't. She's visiting them on Sunday.

Popular TV

1 Read the article. Write the headings for each section in the correct place.

| Watch on your smartphone | Watch free shows on your computer | Watch on your TV |

Great TV through the Internet

Today you can watch great TV through the Internet. You can watch new shows or reruns from around the world.

1 _____

You don't have a smart TV? That's OK. Get a streaming media player. It's a small box, and it's not very expensive. Connect it to your TV, and you can watch shows from the Internet through your TV. You can find good shows through on-demand services. Some services only allow you to watch the most recent episodes. Other services let you watch whole seasons of your favorite shows.

2 _____

Some TV networks allow you to watch their TV shows online for free. Go to the websites of these networks. Look for live streams or past episodes. There are some commercials, but they are usually short.

3 _____

Do you want to take your shows with you everywhere you go? No problem. You can download apps to your smartphone. Search for apps from TV networks or on-demand services. You can watch the shows on a bus, or on a train, or while you are exercising at the gym!

> TV is almost 100 years old! Here are some important dates in the history of television.
> - **1920s** first TV sets
> - **1930s** first TV commercial
> - **1940s** first sitcom, first color TV sets
> - **1950s** first reality show
> - **1960s** first satellite TV

2 Read the article again. Then answer the questions.

1 Are reality shows new? _No, they aren't._

2 Do free online shows have commercials? _____

3 Can you watch reruns online? _____

4 How can you watch TV shows on a bus? _____

5 What can you connect to your TV to watch shows through the Internet? _____